My First Animal Library

Moose

by Cari Meister

Bullfrog Books

Ideas for Parents and Teachers

Bullfrog Books let children practice reading informational text at the earliest reading levels. Repetition, familiar words, and photo labels support early readers.

Before Reading

- Discuss the cover photo. What does it tell them?

- Look at the picture glossary together. Read and discuss the words.

Read the Book

- "Walk" through the book and look at the photos. Let the child ask questions. Point out the photo labels.

- Read the book to the child, or have him or her read independently.

After Reading

- Prompt the child to think more. Ask: Have you ever seen a moose? Were you surprised by its size?

Bullfrog Books are published by Jump!
5357 Penn Avenue South
Minneapolis, MN 55419
www.jumplibrary.com

Library of Congress Cataloging-in-Publication Data

Names: Meister, Cari, author.
Title: Moose / by Cari Meister.
Description: Minneapolis, MN : Jump!, Inc., [2018]
Series: My first animal library | "Bullfrog Books are published by Jump!" | Audience: Ages 5-8.
Audience: K to grade 3. | Includes bibliographical references and index.
Identifiers: LCCN 2017043517 (print)
LCCN 2017041719 (ebook)
ISBN 9781624967597 (e-book)
ISBN 9781624967580 (hardcover : alk. paper)
Subjects: LCSH: Moose—Juvenile literature.
Classification: LCC QL737.U55 (print) | LCC QL737.U55 M37225 2018 (ebook) | DDC 599.65/7—dc23
LC record available at https://lccn.loc.gov/2017043517

Editor: Jenna Trnka
Book Designer: Leah Sanders

Photo Credits: NuttyNu/Shutterstock, cover; Jukka Jantunen/Shutterstock, 1; Darryl Brooks/Shutterstock, 3; Eduard Kyslynskyy/Shutterstock, 4; twildlife/iStock, 5; Gary Gray/iStock, 6–7, 23tr; MEGiordano _ Photography/iStock, 8–9; Eric Isselee/Shutterstock, 9; Don Johnston/Alamy, 10–11, 23mr; Minden Pictures/SuperStock, 12–13, 23tl; Matthew Jacques/Shutterstock, 14; John Mahan/Design Pics/Getty, 15; Mats Lindberg/iStock, 16; Imfoto/Shutterstock, 17; Werner Bollmann/Getty, 18–19, 23bl; Victoria Ditkovsky/Shutterstock, 20–21; S.J. Krasemann/Getty, 22; Richard Seeley/Shutterstock, 23br; Sergey Petrov/Shutterstock, 24.

Printed in the United States of America at Corporate Graphics in North Mankato, Minnesota.

Table of Contents

A Good Swimmer

It is hot.

It is buggy.

What is a
moose to do?

Go for a swim!

A moose is a
good swimmer.

It dives for plants.

leg

Moose are in
the deer family.

They are the largest.

Look at its long legs.

deer

Walking in
forests is easy.

They eat tall plants.

In fall, moose
look for mates.

Bulls fight
for a cow.

It is winter.
Bulls lose
their antlers.

antlers

They will grow back bigger.

Walking in
snow is hard.

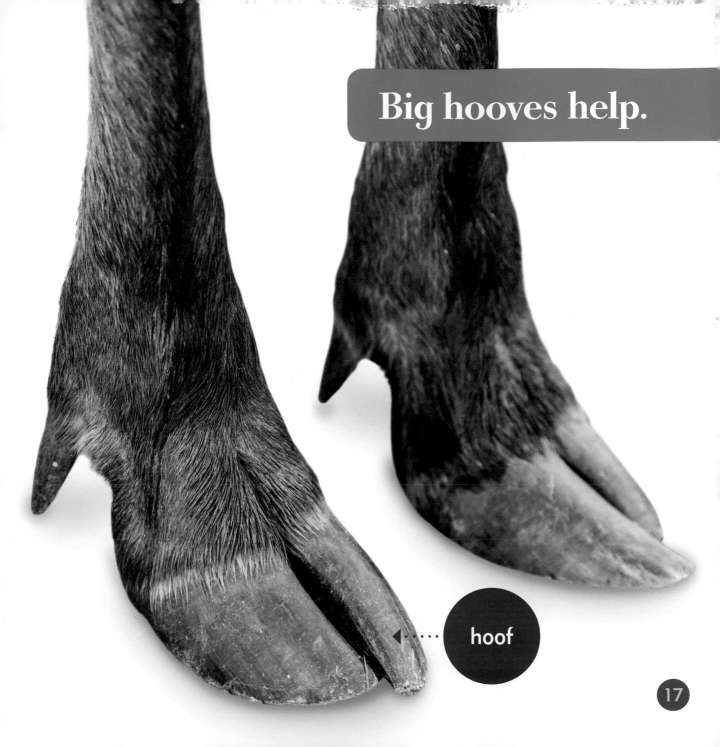

Big hooves help.

hoof

In spring, a cow gives birth.

She has one or two calves.

The calves grow up.
They live on their own.

Parts of a Moose

antlers
A bull uses his antlers to scare off or fight another bull.

bell
The bell is the big flap of skin under a moose's throat. Scientists don't know its purpose; perhaps it's used to attract a mate.

hoof
Each hoof is large. They help support a moose's weight in snow or mud.

legs
Long legs help moose walk through forests and tall snow.

Picture Glossary

bulls
Male moose.

dives
Plunges headfirst into water.

calves
Young moose.

forests
Large areas covered with trees and plants.

cow
A female moose.

mates
Breeding pairs of animals.

Index

To Learn More

Learning more is as easy as 1, 2, 3.

1) Go to www.factsurfer.com

2) Enter "moose" into the search box.

3) Click the "Surf" button to see a list of websites.

With factsurfer.com, finding more information is just a click away.